C000148053

LAT

Andrew Greig is a Scottish writer living in Edinburgh and Orkney. He has written seven novels including *In Another Light* (Weidenfeld & Nicolson), *That Summer* (Faber & Faber) and *The Return of John Macnab* (Quercus). His non-fiction books, on a variety of subjects, include *Summit Fever* (Canongate); *You Know What You Could Be: Tuning into the 1960s* (Quercus), with Mike Heron; *Preferred Lies: A Journey to the Heart of Scottish Golf* (Weidenfeld & Nicolson); and the much-loved *At the Loch of the Green Corrie* (Quercus), a fishing quest in Assynt in memory of his friend and mentor Norman MacCaig. His prose titles are cherished by many for their emotional candour, humanity and enjoyment of storytelling and adventure. Yet the heart of his life's work lies in nine volumes of poetry, including *Found at Sea* (Polygon); *Getting Higher: The Complete Mountain Poems* (Polygon) and *This Life, This Life: New and Selected Poems 1970–2006* (Bloodaxe). His collection *The Order of the Day* (Bloodaxe) was a Poetry Book Society choice.

LATER THAT DAY

Andrew Greig

Polygon

First published in Great Britain in 2020 by
Polygon, an imprint of Birlinn Ltd.

Birlinn Ltd
West Newington House
10 Newington Road
Edinburgh EH9 1QS

www.polygonbooks.co.uk

9 8 7 6 5 4 3 2 1

ISBN 978 1 84697 518 9

British Library Cataloguing-in-Publication Data
A catalogue record for this book is available
from the British Library.

Typeset in Verdigris MVB by Polygon, Edinburgh
Printed and bound by TJ International, Padstow

CONTENTS

III. FROM THE OTHER SIDE
OF THE WORLD

IV. THE WAY TO WAREBETH BEACH

To one and all

I.

AN END TO WAITING

A CAST-IRON ROSE
(Simmerdim at Kisumu, Orkney)

Is that it, then?
To live is to be connected
like the cast-iron rose
to the watering can
inclined in Janet's hand?

Lagavullin flowing among friends,
moonrise over Scapa.
We may not exist
in quite the way we think we do.
Spray collects in leaves,
drips down to parched ground.
Ah, speak for yourself, Calum!

Laughter and moonrise.
Salt-tattered roses bloom.
Had our evenings been more solemn
they would not have been as true.

AND THE WORLD SAYS (A-SIDE)

And the world at daybreak says,
Hold me. Take me back.
Why whinge when I never left your side,
and my hand – invisible, it's true – never ceased
to steer your elbow as you write?

And the world at midnight says,
If it helps, I am the lover's tears
moistening your chest, yon tireless thrush
pouring its heart out in the rain.
You are parched amid such waters?

Listen to me, beloved,
this embrace began when you were born.
I am the sleep you woke from,
the woods you walk through,
the path that grows over when you are gone.

DAY OF THE DOUBLE DUVET

Raise those blinds! The high hills are gone,
mist unrolls and stops above the bungalows
as though cloud lifted its skirts not to
bedraggle them with man-made tosh,
then parts and offers up an *opening*:

and that's it, isn't it? Every day you try (most days
you forget to try, and those days never really dawned
and you lie down at the end of a non-event)
to find a way into what's out there,
so it is no longer out there
and something has been turned *inside out*
like that thing your beloved does with the double duvet:
reverses the cover, dives in headfirst,
feels for the furthest corners and
gripping them emerges.

Watch and learn, man, learn and watch
the sort of ploy women have done all your life,
nonchalant, as though it is self-evident how
one removes bloodstains, separates yolk from white,
when to speak and when to stay silent,
tipping speech into silence and back again
till there is only clarity and sun-yellow in a quiet kitchen
and how to
finish off button thread, or undo buttons
then touch here and here   like this   so light.

So she takes her grasp to the duvet, matches corner to corner,
does that shrugging-off-quick-fluttering thing
and the cover has rolled down the duvet like a fog,
the right way out again.
                              It's a lesson,
a domestic conjuror's reveal
where what has been revealed is not the knack
but she who now stands shaking out the whole,
hair flustered, feet grounded, slightly flushed
as though just back from a successful duck-shoot
or a quick trawl round the charity shops,
the pattern of her being
turned right side out and bright again.

And that's it, show's over.
Now all you have to do is live in it.
Look out the window! Each day you ache to find
some way through this fog within your head,
to emerge with the far corners of the moors
gripped in your eye,
                              and the heart
does the unsayable thing that restores the right way out.
Well may you smile, smoothing out, distributing
self into world, buttoning down the last line.

AND THE WORLD SAYS (B-SIDE)

Who is the one you wake beside
but me in my most pleasing guise –
quick limbs, lips and witty hands,
moving parts that after all these years
still beat your heart like a bodhrán?

Loose your grip on the rush-hour strap,
gaze at the human traffic around you,
each grid-locked in its cage of light –
who could say it is not so,
that I will not leave you, have never let you go?

MORNING TSUNAMI

Waters have risen behind the curtains, beyond
this city, outside the body and within.
They have come for you and everyone,
forcing up through floorboards, shifting
those sandbags stacked around the heart.

Why are they rising? Oh for God's sake
why would they not,
these tumultuous waters of a wave
the size of the world,
oncoming through you, my waking friend?

A LATE REPLY

Wake in the night
Reach for the switch

The book opens
    on words by a friend
        resurrecting a moment
        many, many years earlier
    when we were
  so we believed
lost in the dark

So long ago
but another country? Really?

If I look up
  I see you now

I need reach no further
    than your book

to grip your hand again

GADGETS

They will say of our times,
They had such great gadgets

In the end none of them did
what they were meant to

and they couldn't stop
making and unmaking them.

REGISTRAR

She looked at the world
as though it had just died,
but not for good.

When we gave up on a heart
she would say
Pass the paddles   Charge   Stand back.
A life twitched and came back to us.

Most of course would die again
within hours or days.
Yet a few would go on to live
long and worthwhile lives,
striding corridors of light.

*

In theatre she made everyone else
look like they were trying.

When she dropped her gloves in the bin,
tried to join our hi-jinks
her white coat stayed buttoned.
She sat on the edge of her seat
yearning for A&E.

In an unguarded moment she once told me
Nothing else comes close
and again spoke truer than she knew.

CREATURE COMFORTS

By its creature comforts shall you know
the creature that comforts itself so,
dozing with TV as light fails,
the human animal made happy by
the beloved frying garlic in the kitchen,
the sports decision overturned – *Yes!* – by technology,
the old dog whiffling in her sleep,
a book of poems wings-down on your chest.

You see your life as from above,
something taken by a passing drone –
the comfort zone, the overgrown garden,
the path you once struggled to keep clear
losing definition – it leads only here,
and you won't be walking it again.

Lost and found on the old settee,
mind, hearing, eyesight, failing somewhat
(though touch never dims, does it?),
you never grasped what's going down here,
nor need to now, not long for
this world you long for more than ever.

Life, that tap-in birdie putt,
bundle of feathers wrapped in hide
perpetually toppling into the hole!
You're here to tell me
it has always been so easy
to miss an open goal.

THE SCALES

She wrote a few fair
poems in her lifetime.
They weighed next to nothing
on worldly scales.

Small wonder
she was dour.

Yet when she had her say
the planet creaked up from its abyss
till the bright and dark pans
were dead level.

Her words must have been
much heavier than they seemed
or our world
that much lighter.

BOTTLE

How did you ever
fit within this body,
come to one morning

and find yourself
fully rigged
in too small a container

on a painted ocean,
sails bulging in no wind,
a name set on your bow?

It is improbable,
though most ingenious,
to be present

in such detail,
set alongside others
in a well-lit place

where gods in their free time
come to gaze and point,
shake their heads in wonder

then go back into the day,
walk by a shifting ocean,
real wind in their restless hair.

AN END TO WAITING

for Lesley

I thought of you, beloved –
without conviction, true –
for thirty years before we met.
Whoever held me, I was holding out
for someone other, something more.
A Hayes Code of the heart insisted
I loved with one foot on the floor.
It was not clever and it was not kind.

My loves – and loves they were,
being all that I was up to then –
were not blind but astigmatic.
Light bent off straight
so often it seemed meant.
This my fault, my twist, my limit,
to be with one, imagining another.
It was not kind, it was not clever.

We met, and you became the one
that I see straight: curious, brave,
joyful, empathic and humane –
I spray adjectives, knowing fine
the merit's yours, the change is mine.
When we love, my foot is off the floor.
You are one I never second-guessed,
the one I wish to die before.

The day I married more than you,
I replied, *I surely do*.
Outside, boats left harbour, people passed.
Like any other, that day would end,
but clear-eyed, apprehensive, glad,
I was complete as we exchanged
gold that circles round the bone,
cushioned briefly by our skin.

II.

WHAT'S IN A NAME

CLIMBING EARLY IN GLENCOE

for Malcolm

We talked of the elementary
particles whizzing through
our dazzled eyes and brain
(that mitt held up against the sun)
without altering anything on their way,
without being altered in any way,
indifferent as the frozen face
we climbed that day on Diamond Buttress.

Ice sprayed from our axes,
the ropes ran freely, front points gripped.
Through the cornice's gleaming quiff
we topped out, still talking Science.
We shook hands then stood a while
out of our heads
by the glittering cairn.
We coiled ropes and set off home.

As we clanked downhill
Mal laughed, *So this means
fundamental things have very little
to do with me or you?*
That day's long gone as he is
yet I think we are sustained
by what passes through
and keeps on going

for ever   so they say.

JIMMY SHAND
Stirling, 1961

The Pits

Yon was music-making Scottish style,
a serious business and damn hard work.
The accordion bulged like a chest expander
across the hidden muscle of his heart.
His polkas were gales trapped in a box.
Kilted to the gills, horn specs black as coal
from the mines he went down at fourteen,
Shand gave it laldy, staring straight ahead,
unsmiling, fingers blurred, only movement
his left heel kicking out the beat.
There's nothing free about expression.
He learned that well from earliest days.
Whatever joy there was in it for him
laboured as his father had, deep down.

The Wonder-box

Banned from the pits for playing strikers' benefits,
Jimmy busked moothie and fiddle, switched to melodeon,
his father's instrument, then full chromatic accordion.
Was it the weight? The volume? The precision?
He had a passion for motorbikes:
wonder-box strapped across his back,
he throttled over Slocht, Black Mount, Shap,
to barn dances and weddings, then cash in sporran,
burned his Norton back to Auchtermuchty.
What did he dream of, barrelling through the dark?
Back in our kitchen, stout Mrs Keay
lowered the needle on his new release, pulled
her silent husband Willie from his chair
and shook it like a chorus girl.

'I see you keep a bee'

Jimmy Shand was very dry. At a Brechin B&B
he requested honey with his toast.
The dour landlady brought a tiny pot.
He inspected it: *I see you keep a bee.*
He lived for his work and his work was music.
Carnegie Hall, Dunfermline or New York, no odds:
he named tune, time signature, then played it.
His audience sat as though at prayer,
heads bowed, sucking sweeties, silently
nodding along to their music-maker.
That hall was crammed with joy, minutely expressed.
The compression of his mouth set off
the hoot of his reels, jigs, strathspeys.
They rightly named a locomotive after him.

The Bluebell Polka

The applause of the night came when
he announced his biggest hit, produced by George Martin,
before taking on a provincial harmony rhythm group
who wore their laughter, horniness and rebellion
on the outside, with their leather jackets –
my kind, my time, my music, that would soon condemn
tweed and dignity to the Museum of Embarrassments,
along with kilts, Brylcreem and self-restraint.
Yet when Jimmy counted in 'The Bluebell Polka',
glee blew through our stolid hall, and bells
shook numberless blue clappers below the miles of trees
that line the taut and narrow road from Tarbert,
flashed on by the biker impassive at the throttle,
connecting high lands to low in one marvellous gale.

SADIE DOG

A lifetime of careering
after gulls that took flight

a blur after squirrels
that always made it up the tree

How you would yelp below
hair raised along your spine
barking at everything beyond your reach

not in the least dismayed

Creature of the earth
this time you have bolted
where we cannot call you back

Death alone has brought you to heel

TRAINING SESSION BELOW WESTER CRAIGLOCKHART

Cold wind and dry branch.
Below Wester Craiglockhart
the field of dreams lies blank.

Onto it run, in assorted strips,
garrulous energies, keen, semi-fit.
They warm up, begin to link
in ways neglected all summer;
pants and chirrups, faint cries and groans,
puffs of breath rise up as they scrum down.
Who knows what goings-on
are going on in there?
How hard these words lock horns!

Some have begun to run
  in broken lines across the field;
    the synaptic ball is deftly flipped
      between the swift, then with abrupt
        side-stepping enjambment
the prize moves back inside again.

You stand absorbed by dummy runs
missed moves   not-so-accidental obstruction
reverse pass   off-load   chip and gather
playful variations with but one aim:
to break down the lock-tight drift defences of our day.

Though they meet no opposition,
shouts ring across the empty stands
when they combine the length of the field;
between the posts one swoops to ground
a muddy full stop.

They warm down, troop off the field
still bantering, arms round shoulders.
Sole spectator, coach, selector,
silent on a wintry peak you stand,
stout conquistador in hefty overcoat,
look at your notes and wonder
how on Earth this season and its nations
will play out.

THE WILD SHIRT

to Val, on her birthday

If Life were a tropical shirt
it would bear no maker's name,
no size, provenance or cleaning instructions.
No symbols of any kind.

The price tag's removed –
after all, it is a present!
Don't worry about the fit:
however big you get

it just gets bigger.
Put it on, friend.
Any label you add now
is your own work.

We know the whole show
ends in charity shops –
meanwhile it's a crime
not to shoot those gorgeous cuffs!

WILLIAM FOWLER IN PADUA

Why go to Padua?
You will learn nothing there
but anatomy and deceit.

I tell you this much
it was a bloody miracle
we got out unflayed.

Peering over the rails
of the *teatro anatómic*,
we learned to sketch the dead,
trust detail, not the old masters:

assignations in the midnight piazza,
a bulge beneath the cloak
and tiny brackets around his mouth
when the Cardinal made promises,
the hush in the dissecting theatre
as our instructors folded back the skin.

At times it was hard not to giggle or throw up.

*

Our lackey Nicolson studied algebra in the mornings
(Let n be the number of heretics in the Inns
Plus 1 for the informer, even Galileo smiled)

God knows what proclivities in the afternoons!
Nights he slept on the floor by the door
rolled in his cloak like a draught excluder.

I sat up late, reworking smutty
Petrarchean verse in Scott's bad Florentine
while the man himself was, how shall I put this,
elsewhere engaged with the Spanish ambassador.

*

The foremost proclaimer of Giordano Bruno's genius
was himself. How we groaned
when he turned up for the position
to find Galileo already had the post.
Only a fool trusts a Venetian.
His pyre was made of green wood –
it burned extra slow.

Dawn found us survivors
not all sweet smelling,
bums on hard pews as we peered down
at the new man on the marble slab
as ripe for unveiling
as the Contessa's sly friend,
her fingernail a scalpel tracing my wrist.

We matriculated in 1591
to study what lay beneath the skin.
In the end we did not graduate
so much as escape,
our jerkins heavy with metal.

I'll say this, friend: back in Embra
for a long time we looked upon the living
the way we had come to regard the dead
within the Palazzo del Bo, in Padua.

LATE KANDINSKY, ANTHEA AND INGRID

*Just as there are enough dead triangles, there are just as many dead
roosters, dead horses or dead guitars.*

Wassily Kandinsky

Every bright thing you look at long and hard enough
   sooner or later oozes black outline
that briefly heightens the colours within.
   As death seeps down from grandparents to parents,

to peer then friend then child,
   and the first body you knew as flesh
within living flesh, goes up in smoke,
   and the next rots in the ground,

it gets so the living are scarcely there,
   like passers-by in early photographs,
ghosts as they go on urgent business.
   The black outline thickens like a waistline.

I want to shed a few pounds of death,
   I think as my bus pass goes unchallenged,
and watch that baby guzzling its demise
   in the guise of a ring-pull dummy.

I am thinking of that Kandinsky retrospective
   at the Tate, one summer in the Eighties, on
one of my below-the-radar trips to London,
   custodianed by Anthea or Ingrid von Essen –

both long dead, which is probably why
   I falter on ascription, scrawl: *Dead woman friend*
as caption for this memory
   where a pale hand indicates how Naturalism

begins its long slog towards Abstraction
   when Death enters the picture (Wassily's bairn
who must not be mentioned, ever) in the second gallery.
   Sheep, clouds, Cossacks, a stoical cow

poised by a river, lances and church, all become
   ringed in black, insistently as a pissed-off child
who believes if he sulks hard enough, the world
   will give him a break, make an exception

so this time ice-cream comes with chocolate sauce,
   and no one has to die. It worked? You stopped?
Of course not! So you'll understand the phase
   when cow, river, Cossacks drop out, as though someone

had taken a paper-punch to canvas, leaving only
   black outline, bullet hole, the shape of a singular
unretrievable absence. In that mode
   you cannot tell one dead friend from another:

their deaths have hollowed out your heart, leaving
   only the shape of their going.
Abstraction is born not from geometry
   but from seeing death ever-present as it is.

That must be Ingrid. I have installed
   her death's head face, near-white Finnish hair –
a sliver of glacier wrapped in black leather,
   blue glittering stare, that blink-and-you-missed-it smile

brief as winter sunlight in Helsinki, into this scene.
   This before our foolish falling out, unresolved
till cancer eased her from the picture
   leaving only the shape of her not being there;

Anth must have stayed home that day, glass
   by glass becoming fuzzy then speechless
till one Xmas morning only a red outline
   lay stretched across the bed.

If the dead were watching – I think not, but we
   do watch on their behalf, as though
their vanishing point makes convincing
   the illusion called 'Real Life' – they'd say

Get a grip, you lucky living bastard,
   and take my arm, as Ingrid did
– Were we? Did we ever? You must be joking –
   that lurid summer in the Eighties, and tug me

past the transition phase, that passage
   of black outline and non-specific grey,
into the space where late Kandinsky blazes
   blue of the sky behind endless sky

against which spindles, prawns, impossibly balancing
   spires, cylinders, moons green, vermillion and yellow
and, yes, black, small globes of black rolling
 down inclined planes of colour, black

as one more abstraction in a colour field:
   The shape of the sound of Moscow's bells,
   Alternative music for mind and senses,
   In love with things but not dependent on them.

Pure ploy! Inexhaustible splendour
   of the presence of absent friends!
Lead me on, Ingrid of the outlines
   who made me write and think harder,

who lived on vitamins and solitude
   too deep to penetrate, whose heart
was radiant and dark as a diamond mine,
   whom I adored but never dared touch,

take me on where jokes and emptiness
   poise precisely in incandescent blue,
then out into the traffic boom again;
   over the spire a quarter moon

is pure Kandinsky, and Ingrid's smile
   drills into my heart as we cross
Trafalgar Square, then onwards to whatever
   will become of me, and her, and us.

III.

FROM THE OTHER
SIDE OF THE WORLD

DAY I
Waiheke Island

Some four years in
found me on the back green birling
arms outstretched
dervish in corduroy
watching the morning blur
then stopped
dead
living
while birch and trike and washing lines turned

A high-pitched ringing
brushed over the trees
stroked the crown of my head
as though I were the ball
casually slung into a roulette wheel
against the flow
slowing
finally falling
into the slot of myself

At the centre of the birling
outcome of a gamble
not of my making
in green dungarees and red sandals
I lowered my arms

and for the first time
grasped
what is being lost and won
from here on in

Sixty years later and none the wiser
still a little shining ball
settled in my slot
in the turning world
with no sense of its turning
but for that ringing
high and faint
there
from finish to start

my father's finger circling his glass on a summer afternoon

LOOKING AT STINKHORN

Pah Homestead, Auckland

I.

Little one, it is not nothing
from which you've come,
bloody head easing through forest floor.

The subterranean has given birth
to an outlandish crown,
raising its head to peek

in wonder at its own arrival.

II.

Rain and decomposing mulch
will sustain you, homely grub,
though kings with greater fanfare
live on little other.

The trees set over you, those grand admonishers,
will outlive you a thousand times.

Be not abashed, red smudge
with the unpromising name;
they will fall, and their rot raise
ten thousand of your cousins.

III.

One week old today, already
your crimson whorls are edged with black.
You're dying as you live.

My hips are stiff, my fingers creak . . .
Sod elegy, my brief companion!
It is not nothing from which you've come

but everything, to which you now return.
Such growing pains, yet how we grasp
our season in the shade!

THINKING ABOUT SAM HUNT AT
KAIPARA HARBOUR

The examined life
has become as it has always been

watching the river run
once in a while jumping in
coming out further downstream

Sitting on the bank drying off
your mind wanders back upstream
where your body can never walk again

Never see those faces again

But you think about them a lot
till it's time to dive in
one last time as the sun gets low

*

Unmet friend, you write as one
who once in a while discerned
the script within the scrawl
then woke to find himself
translated

Your words speak to me in Dunedin
where my late evening is
my grandchildren's morning

They're just getting up
I'm heading for bed

*

Some martyrdom, Sam

Hammering in nails each evening
pulling out nails each morning
climbing stiffly down from the Cross

It's a good life
Damn where is that donkey
How goes the testament today

Entering Jerusalem again

EXPLORER (AT KAREKARE)

'Follow the stream of senses to its source'

In truth there's no way back from here,
no well-stocked camp, no waiting comrades.

Part the jungle then the reeds,
push past your mentors' remains.
The native bearers quit long ago –
why risk their health and sanity for you?
Dress your own wounds, look after your feet,
go easy on the booze.

Follow the muddy, least promsing river.
You anticipate a great shining lake
from which all love's waters run?
A clear spring rising in the heart?
Anything but this sudden end
in black sand, cliffs and ocean.

Whoever thought it all ends here,
with terror crashing onto wonder?
Give in, give up, give over, kneel
on Karekare beach under the stars.
Be a match struck in thunderous night,
sole witness to your final smile.

SETTLERS

The Pah Homestead, Auckland

I.

What does a man need to start with
Fire   shelter   washbowl   chopper
Most of all belief or at least curiosity
just how far can he take this

At the end of the day
bed   washbowl   chamberpot   mate
Barred door and exhaustion make
sleep blank as starless sky

What does a woman need to settle
Fire   shelter   washbowl   chopper
Most of all belief or at least hope
her steps will make a path appear

At the end of the day
bed   washbowl   chamberpot   mate
Warm night in chill surroundings
These new stars may be good

*

Fifty acres per soul brought us here
Those who owned only a body that works
a weaving loom   a two-handed saw   a good eye

Those who had their letters and numbers
the stewpot of their Faith salt-stained but sound
wrapped in a mother's shawl

'The promised land is two weeks through the jungle
Between the turtle headland and the white spit
All yours if you can clear it, friend'

Well stuff my boots
We'd best get going
afore we grow ony thinner

*

The early settlers cleared wilderness
planted parklands that made sense to them
What do we do on leaving home

but remake it more expansively
Morton Bay Fig   Kauri   Olive   Spanish Oak
Tui   Fantail   Blackbird   Silvereye

Carriages lurch through the forest
up the rutted driveway past specimen trees
towards the Italianate Homestead on the hill

jellies   ice cream   kumara   biscuits
mutton   pork   takahē   beef
roast chicken most popular with Maori guests
Whale-oil lamps lit yellow along the porch

new-woven hats and fresh-shaved chins
Calloused hands scrubbed smooth

toast our growing numbers
all who have made it so far
Let us make the old country again but better

Let this be our new tradition

11.
Some prospered   many went bust
Slow learners went bust again
Quitters left for Australia
(raising the average IQ of both lands)

Cheers when first children born here
Some died quickly but enough did not
We laid out our cemetery high on the ridge
above a town that did not yet exist

After all this is a land of opportunity not immortality

*

On a rocker on decking sawn and planed by his own hands
an early settler squints past his cataracts
We began with stockades then worked on out

Cracks knuckles stiffened with labour
fingers lost to the saw   thumbs spread by hammers
Beasts want pasture and pasture needs fences
So the farm grows   well mostly it overgrows
given half a chance
yet our beasts taste good and please the eye
Can just see them grazing at the forest's edge

The first necessity of new lands
    survivors
The second necessity
    honest surveyors

After that come storyteller and lawyer
for deeds are perpetuated by deeds

*

It takes thirty years' hard labour to make a farm

If you get lucky
you may live five more
sit in the shade jawing with toothless pals
watch your children working

They'll settle elsewhere and never see these trees again
the bala bala   Sandra's willow greiting by the loch

Ach the memory of her strong hands
planting out and thinning   at night in my hair
Ach the memory of her

Folk will say, *Those are settlers' trees*
They must have had great faith and generosity
Mostly energy to burn and heartache
Watch your children thrive and wonder
will they sell the farm

III.
In time trees grew great into their space
Sawmills squared timber to build
more houses where trees had been

Civilisation is built by hammer and nails
shiploads of nails
though a good carpenter goes a long way

In early days our handshakes gripped like tenon joints

Newspapers make best mulch for English roses
Obituaries   Notices   Editorials   Maori Wars
They fought well and dug in trenches

Unwinnable
We signed the treaty at Waitangi
took it from there

*

The war against entropy
is a losing battle
but see what waging it has made

Long-tailed bat   rose parakeet   green turtle   copper moth
muskets   migrations   treaties   songs made new
manly sports and art
In time stadia and galleries
ever more complex preposterous dazzling works

The Great Watch may be running down
but it passes the time
making ever more intricate
watches

IV.
In time news from here exceeds news from home
Build better harbours   more boats come
Build jetties so after the nightmare journey
months vomiting cramped dark below deck
alongside our animals
howling   grunting   squealing   barking
precious as any human   for that time all beasts together
so we may step ashore without wading through mud
Raise glasses to our parents
who never made it
but prayed one day we would
drink what is roughly beer
under unfamiliar stars

*

Home fades but is not lost
It stays on in the old songs
Winter festivals at the hottest time of the year
Lighting candles when the light is longest

It is in the warm wind from the North
flowing over our arms asking
how long does it take
till this is entirely real
and our bones know
they are on the right side of the world

Mind you only children know this is entirely real

From here on, we are settlers
who will never entirely settle
and that keeps us busy
roads   farms   dams   wineries
so we can put off all reckoning
till our breath comes shallow and infrequent
till the carriage brakes outside the homestead
till the boat bumps the dark jetty

Friend it is time to disembark

v.

Being born is leaving home forever and a day
Fire   shelter   washbowl   mate
Let them bloom and drop their petals

Washbowl and chamberpot cleaned by rain
Fire burns down the shack
Next time build in stone

Now mate lies deep by mate
their children look at each other and say
Best get going afore we grow ony thinner

Moreover my mother sang at the stove
a song of her own devising
for the country she had settled in

   Far across the firmament the floating sausage blows
   He seeks his little frying pan the only home he knows

and though she is long gone
while her children walk in light

she is not far wrong

IV.

THE WAY TO WAREBETH BEACH

RETURN TO THE GREEN CORRIE

for Ron, Brian and Liz: the Lost Poets

Our early efforts, bubblings from scree.
Feeder streams conjoin and fall
as though breaking silence were enough.

A lochan gathered among stones.
The exit burn
babbled away over shallows.

Meanwhile MacCaig,
his wife dying then dead,
hirpled on towards lucidity,

down into the gloaming
his burdensome heart visible at last,
slumped over his shoulder like a shot stag.

IN A DRY GORGE (CRETE)

We walk each day
in the shadow of the valley

so occupied by thought and conversation
our gesturing hands

fail to grasp
the implication of our situation

The light that pours down behind these crags
this waterless gorge carved out by water

We block light like sundial spikes
make time and tell

how dark the shadow that travels with us
the radiance it takes to cast it

CLOUDS AT SEA OFF COLONSAY

Clouds slide back
  their raggedy hatches

How human, we think
  easing away from the dock

they look peaceful
  and their hearts are thunderous

Sometimes I wonder
  how they can stay up

what we will do with
  such cargo as ours

ON BROUGH OF BIRSAY, ORKNEY

Weeds stretched in the current
clinging to our bit of rock
with so much flapping and weaving
we must be getting somewhere

She turned to me
We also serve
to mark tide's turn

Today the water is so clear
between Birsay and the mainland
even at flood tide we can see
the causeway underneath

Our race is not yet run
My love who can say
we may not yet know better days

LANDING

When the children phone in
to tick us from their to-do list,
suggest we might get out more,
we say, *Uh-huh   Mmm   Love you too*
and when we put the phone down
see we've stopped winding
the clocks on Sunday mornings.

Do they know we just don't care?
Let light and dust fall as they will.
Our days have simplified
to getting up the stair.

Our world is made up in this house
as it was when we were bairns
and all that mattered was at hand.
Soon none of this will be ours;
we meet on the landing,
pause for breath and then
regard each other face to face again.

THE OLD CODGERS

If experience counts for anything,
don't come to Glasgow without a coat.
Soaked, I round the corner off Byres Road,
where under the awning, in autumn rain,
at pavement tables outside the Ubiquitous Chip,
the Codgers sit wreathed in mufflers and roll-ups.

Eric Plectrum sees me coming, waves his stick.
Handshakes all round, introductions and reminders
we are the ones who got off with it
and now sit wrapped against the raw
as young people pass in shirt sleeves, still in the game.
Our hair is silver, gone or grey, and it is clear
by our jackets (not fleeces), buttoned shirts, sweaters,
laced shoes or battered cowboy boots (not trainers),
we are onlookers, not players.

Smoke and laughter wreath us round.
We sip slowly (the fast drinkers are long gone).
Names are summonsed, praised, some cursed
but most forgiven, glimpsed again in a pause
as someone raises scarred fingers to deliver the punchline
of a yarn not entirely funny, the way we come
to see the whole shebang: funny, but not entirely.
Stories of bands, shows, crash-pads – let us commemorate
joints the size of trumpets, minds blown
by music, home-brew and bad acid!

Good gigs, bad gigs, catastrophic gigs!
Women lost, departed, glorious, unkind!
She was a viper, God rest her.

Our cause is just to sit here longer.
Sometimes young people drop by,
warming us like mobile outdoor heaters,
my Leo with his Blues and call centre,
Brian's daughter just back from earthquakes,
radiant, in love, ready to head off again.
They won't own homes until we're gone
and we are edging towards the exit like guests
ready to slip away before the bill's presented.

Lightness and laughter, amid the gravity of our situation!
Children grown, mortgage cleared, ambition
a huge umbrella bumping through the crowd,
more burden than it's worth, slightly absurd,
finally abandoned who knows when.
How very little matters now
but sitting in shelter with each other.
I raise my glass of some new lager
I don't like but have drunk too much of,
to toast these weightless afternoons together:

we have become what we least expected,
a bunch of old codgers getting quietly pissed
at pavement tables off Byres Road,

with nowhere else we want to be
as late afternoon wears into evening
and Glasgow rain pools on the awning above,
runs down past our hats and shoulders,
like death, still just missing us.

TOWARDS THE END OF THE FEAST

The best way to bear
that flaming pud
signalling the latter stages of our feast

is not with Kenneth McKellar's rictus grin
nor the fugitive grimace
that passed for a smile among men.

The best way to carry
between steamer and table
the dark fruit of our last course:

let slip the clay-white platter
and in the moment before
the mess on the floor,

the crash, the stricken faces,
know to your fingertips
the joy of letting go,

lightness rushing up
to greet you like an old pal.
Thus did my father on his last Christmas,

from hands that once had eased
many a bairn into the world,
look up at us, with the smile of a child.

IN THE FIELDS OF OBLIVION

My parents lie
in the fields of oblivion
neither awake nor asleep
stirring as the wind blows
each time I think on them

There were times the red mist descended
The first summer we were in the new house
your sister must have been asleep
your father was working in the garden
I took off my clothes and stood at the window

Now his hand lies spread on hers
at the far corners of the Earth
I cannot see ripe grain
bow down across the fields
as other than her smile that afternoon

THE WAY TO WAREBETH BEACH

It is the way grass bends over puddles and rutted track,
yields to the wind then springs back,
shaking out last seeds as the season ends.

It is the way the track runs from graveyard to rough grazing
where clover and faded sea pinks quiver,
the sea charging forward yet getting no closer.

It is the way the light grows more lurid,
dark clouds over Hoy making blue lighter,
pressing dark into early night,

and the volume of waves and the volume of wind
pour in through eyes and ears
till all is high water at Warebeth.

*

Seaweed and salt frazzle the soft
linings of the nose, neural pathways register
the way a black-backed gull moves
into the gale without beating its wings.
A sleight of weight and tilt of feathers,
it passes through the dilated sun,
turns black, emerges lit red,
pivots on one wing
        then much faster slides downwind
back through the sun and out again
to show what practice and a backing wind can do.

*

It is the way surges keep rolling in, mount the shallows,
unzip along the seam spilling white foam feathers.
None of this has ever exactly repeated itself, not once,

for otherwise the world would be static and a trap
instead of being beyond control and comprehension
and suitable for living in, given you too are beyond

comprehension and control – the silhouette of a notion
passes through the sun, to the effect
being alive is not the riddle but its answer

as though the Divine were Hendrix in bandana and loons
smashing his Stratocaster into the galactic columns
listening intently to the howl

*

The sun has gone and light is going fast.
The wind is cold and it is time to go home.
The dog drags her muzzle from sheep shit in grass.

The path looked at this way is the same path but different,
not the path of going but the path of returning.
Spent grass springs up, bows again along the verges.
You would think after all these years the wind
would have arrived at its destination and settled down
like an old dog in its basket.

You open the car door, Sadie struggles into the back seat.
Up front, you believe you are driving
even as you witness yourself driving
away from the beach and the track to the sea.
You believe you are going home, as though you were not
already home, as if here were somewhere else

and now is a time where we do things differently.
In the mirror the path fades into the dark,
and the metalled road is near-dark but you won't
switch on the lights just yet,
for your eyes have adjusted and this dimness is just right
and the way to the sea and the way home

remain two and the same,
the only way open to you,
not so hard to follow through gathering dark.

ACKNOWLEDGEMENTS

Some of these poems first appeared in *The Dark Horse*; *Northwords Now*; *Horns & Wings & Stabiliser Things: The Lost Poets* (Polygon, 2020); *Le Simplegadi* (University of Udine) and *Scotia Extremis*, edited by Andy Jackson and Brian Johnstone (Luath Press).

Warmest thanks to the Wallace Arts Trust, University of Otago, the Pah Homestead in Auckland and Liam McIlvanney for the hospitality, New Zealand experiences and writing time that led to many of these poems.